KT-155-719

Horse Tips
&
Pony Tales

ILPH

Important message regarding horse welfare from the ILPH

Should you suspect there is anything physically wrong with your horse please do not use any of these tips as a substitute for calling your vet. In many instances the ILPH is publishing the thoughts of others and does not guarantee the safety or effectiveness of these tips.

Published by EAE Creative Colour on behalf of International League for the Protection of Horses, Anne Colvin House, Snetterton, Norfolk NR16 2LR

First published 2000

ISBN 0-9539326-0-5

A catalogue record for this book is available from the British Library

All rights reserved. No part of this publication may be reproduced, stored in a retrieval system, or transmitted, in any form or by any means, electronic, mechanical, photocopying, recording or otherwise, without the prior permission of the Publishers

Copyright © International League for the Protection of Horses (ILPH) 2000
Compiled by Phil Spiby and Sue Pidduck from an original concept by Jeremy James
Designed and typeset by Postscript Communications Ltd
Illustrated by Trevor Baker, BDI Creative
Printed and bound by EAE Creative Colour

Foreword

The original concept for this book came from Jeremy James who
has worked as an Overseas Consultant for the ILPH for many
years. The ILPH are often faced with situations in the developing
world where considerable ingenuity and lateral thinking are
needed to improve horse welfare in spartan conditions. You will
find a sprinkling of Jeremy's tips throughout the book.

Horse Tips and Pony Tales contains tips and anecdotes from
many ILPH personnel, its Field Officers and farm staff.
It has been compiled over a number of years and also includes
contributions from the general public and well-known
personalities. We are very grateful to all of the contributors
for having taken the time to write in.

The ILPH have been performing important work for horse
welfare since its foundation in 1927. In the United Kingdom it
runs six farms dedicated to the recovery and rehabilitation of
horses with over 300 equines in care at any one time. Full-time
ILPH Field Officers, nearly all ex-mounted policemen, investigate
cases of cruelty and neglect, inspect markets and ports and check
the 1700 rehabilitated horses and ponies currently rehomed
through the ILPH loan scheme. In the developing world, the
ILPH runs educational and training courses to combat the
major causes of equine suffering and help the owners to
help themselves.

The focus is on providing education, as knowledge lives on after your departure, and using locally available materials to establish sustainable and permanent solutions to problems.

Thanks to the generosity of the EAE Creative Colour Ltd who have taken on the cost of production – it means by buying this book you have contributed to the ILPH's valuable work. I would hope that, having read it, you might also like to continue supporting the work, which makes such a difference to the welfare of horses around the world.

HRH The Princess Royal GCVO
President of the ILPH

Contents

Chapter 1 ~ page 1
A healthy horse is a happy horse

Chapter 2 ~ page 11
A few words of wisdom

Chapter 3 ~ page 23
A law unto themselves

Chapter 4 ~ page 29
I remember when...

Chapter 5 ~ page 51
Rhyme and reason

Chapter 6 ~ page 61
And finally...

*Riding is the simple process
of keeping the horse between you
and the ground.*

Anon

Chapter One

A healthy horse is a happy horse

Gorse code

I had a tip from a good Romany Gypsy who was an
authority on horses and kept some beautiful ponies.
He told me that if your horse or pony is ever lacking in
appetite or generally run down, go and find some gorse.
Only use the new growth which is found at the top of the
bush - you'll have to wear strong gardening gloves to avoid
the vicious thorns - then tie it in a small bundle and feed
it to your horse or pony by tying it tightly to the ring in
its stable. I have tried this with a sick horse and
it worked!

Dave Guy
ILPH Field Officer

*Tip also sent in by David Nicholson, Racehorse Trainer and
Eileen Gillen, Farm Manager, ILPH Belwade Farm.*

No flies on him

Choose a corner of a paddock and slit seed lemongrass or citronella into it. Horses won't graze lemongrass or citronella grass, but they'll walk on it and as they do so they'll bruise it and the scent that rises will keep flies away. (Hot climates only.)

Jeremy James
ILPH Overseas Consultant

Rub him up the right way

The old paraffin rag rubbed over the horse's body keeps the flies away and also puts a good sheen on the coat.

John Pearson
ILPH Field Officer

Know your onions!

Hanging an onion in the stable or horsebox helps prevents colds and viruses – an old wives' tale, but it has been proven to work.

Eileen Gillen
Farm Manager, ILPH Belwade Farm

Welcome to the world

If you want your foal to grow up to be sensible, fearless and
humanised, it is imperative that you spend the first hour of his
life with him. Touch him everywhere, pick up his feet and put
your fingers in his mouth. This will 'imprint' on his brain and
nothing you do later in his education will frighten him.

Lead him by his mane with someone gently pushing
him along from behind. This can be a real life-saver in
an emergency with an adult horse.

Mrs Susan Eckholdt
The Equuleus Falabella Stud

Controlled eating

This one will sound odd I know, but train your pony to eat on
command! I have a Highland who is always thinking of his
stomach. Because we have to restrict his grazing, we often lead
him out to graze in hand. He is also led out with riders, both
children and a man with learning difficulties. Using a pressure
halter, I have taught him the command 'Findlay, Eat!'. I use
'Walk on' when I want him to stop feeding. Now he does not try
and eat when being led, but waits for the command. (And if it
works for a Highland it will work for anything!)

Elizabeth Lovick
Orkney

4

Heavy horse

Pick up a foal when he's young and keep picking him up. Pick him up as often as you can and he'll get used to it. He'll learn to trust you – particularly if you don't drop him. When he's fully grown he'll still think you can pick him up and you'll have a quiet horse for ever.

Jeremy James
ILPH Overseas Consultant

5

Tails tell tales

In many cases, posture can be linked to behaviour and
a horse or pony tail can give you a lot of information about
the way he or she may react to certain situations.
A tightly clamped tail often indicates nervousness and
sensitivity to movement or noise behind. A loose 'spaghetti'
tail may mean that the horse finds it difficult to engage
its hindquarters.

Circling the tail gently several times in both directions
can help to loosen or 're-connect' the tail. This simple and highly
effective technique is used worldwide by many endurance riders
to help release tension from their horse's backs before, during
and after competition.

Try this by standing to the side of the left hindquarter
to avoid being trodden on or kicked, and cup your left hand
under the top of the dock. Place your right hand on the end
of the tail bone and lift the tail gently but firmly. With
your knees slightly bent, circle the tail several
times in both directions.

You may find that the tail is looser when moving in a
particular direction, which generally correlates to the side the
horse is most supple on. As the tail circles become more even
over time, you should find that the horse becomes more
balanced under saddle.

If people pass comment, just smile and tell them that you are
simply winding up your equine friend to get him going!

Sarah Fisher
TTEAM Practitioner

 6

Fixing up a date

Horses like dates – the edible kind. They provide instant energy and refresh a hot, thirsty horse. They spit the pips out too!

Jeremy James
ILPH Overseas Consultant

An end to cracked hooves

If you horse has soft, crumbly feet and they crack no matter what you do, this can be a real worry. Shoes often don't stay on and the hooves look ugly and uncared for.

Buy some Formalin from your local chemists or chemical supplier and paint it on the soles of the feet and on the walls just up to the nail holes. This will harden the hooves and stop them crumbling. Formalin is simply an aqueous solution of formaldehyde which is a preservative and disinfectant.

Kat Koukourakis
Ex Head Girl, ILPH Cherry Tree Farm

Shell out for your horse

Next time you go to the seaside, collect half a sackful of
sea shells and crush them, by running over them in a car for
example. Tip the ground-up shells into a water butt and your
horse will never get a starey coat nor have bad teeth, and
his feet will be better too.

Jeremy James
ILPH Overseas Consultant

A swell solution

If your horse acquires itself a swollen knee or hock from a
bruise, wrapping a large cabbage leaf (preferably spring cabbage)
will help to reduce the swelling. Just watch out that the horse
doesn't eat it!

Eileen Gillen
Farm Manager, ILPH Belwade Farm

Love potion

Rub a little of your favourite scent on the belly of a mare
as soon as she has foaled. And dab a little on yourself. The foal
will get to know that scent and associate it with his mother.
It will remember it all its life, believing that the scent means
security. Years later it will follow you whenever you or any
other person – or horse – happens to be wearing it.

Jeremy James
ILPH Overseas Consultant

Wave sweet-itch goodbye!

If your horse or pony suffers from sweet-itch, this solution, made with cheap and easily obtainable ingredients, really does work.

Ingredients

Vinegar: 4 tbsp
Methylated spirit: 1tbsp
Citronella oil: 33 ml (available at local chemists)
Strong tea (cooled) 1 cup
Make up to 2 litres with water.

To make it:

Put the vinegar with the methylated spirit and citronella oil, mix them together and then pour in the tea. Mix thoroughly, then add water to make up to 2 litres.

To use it:

Buy a spray bottle from your local garden centre and use it to spray the solution all over the horse's body once or twice daily, particularly before sunset. Avoid the horse's eyes, and do not spray in open wounds as it can cause irritation.

Before you know it the scabs will heal and the mane and tail will even grow back. If you start treating at the beginning of the midge season, your horse may suffer no symptoms of sweet-itch at all.

Kat Koukourakis
Ex Head Girl, ILPH Cherry Tree Farm

Chapter Two

A few words of wisdom

No more saddle sores

Whenever you have been riding for few hours on a hot summer's day, loosen the girth before you get off your horse, but then leave the saddle where it is. Get a bucket of cold water. Undo the girth, take the saddle off and immediately slosh the water over the horse's back. You'll never get a heat bump again.

Jeremy James
ILPH Overseas Consultant

John Hislop
The Times, 1987

On the turf there is only one rightful king – the racehorse. And if he is not served in the manner due to him, neither he nor his kingdom will prosper.

Sir Peter O'Sullevan
Racing Commentator and Journalist

Mind your language

I often hear people 'clicking' all the time to their horses.
If used in the wrong context, this can be confusing for the horse.
There are four simple commands that a horse can easily learn
if they are only used at the appropriate time.

'Clicking' means 'Forwards', ie move forwards or move faster
and be more active.

'Back' means 'Move backwards'. Teach this by pushing the
horse's shoulder and saying 'Back'. Never click to move your
horse backwards.

'Over' means 'Move the quarters over'. Teach this by waving
at the hindquarter or pushing/prodding the quarter gently
with your hand.

'Whoa' means 'Stop'. This is a very important command,
because your horse must learn to stand still. Teach it by
touching the shoulder or quarter if the horse tries to
step forwards or backwards respectively.

Teach your horse these commands and it won't just be
much easier to handle him, but it will also help with teaching
him to turn on the forehand, rein back, square halts and
move actively.

Kat Koukourakis
Ex Head Girl, ILPH Cherry Tree Farm

Pick up your feet!

When teaching a young or difficult horse to pick up its feet,
gently squeeze the chestnut on the relevant leg.

Liz Hatten
ILPH Mobile Promotions Officer

Milk sap

To get a real top polish on your
saddle, buff it with milk.

Jeremy James
ILPH Overseas Consultant

A good horseman?

In the depths of winter of war 1916, a mare floundered into
a bog. Up to her belly in mud the mare struggled frantically to
free herself and then gave up. Her rider, a dispatch corporal,
realising she had lost the will to go on, slipped off her back,
swum through the mud, unzipped his fly and piddled as hard
as he could into her ear. The horse shook her head violently,
struck out with her front legs, fought wildly to free herself,
scrambled out of the bog, then galloped off back in the direction
from which she'd come – alone. Whatever happened to the
dispatch rider, history doesn't relate.

Jeremy James
ILPH Overseas Consultant

We can work it out

Don't get even, get off! Sometimes horses can really try your patience, but losing your temper doesn't benefit either of you, and you'll only regret it later. Rather than risk undoing all the hard work you've put in already, or destroying the trust and friendship you've built up, go and work out your frustrations on the muck-heap instead by giving it a good tidy-up.

Karen Bush
Equestrian author, journalist and riding instructor

Training racehorses is about observation. They can tell you nothing but they can't lie either, so if you are sufficiently observant everything is there.

Sir Mark Prescott Bt
Racehorse Trainer

15

Attention all carriage drivers!

For Carriage Drivers, a suit carrier is very useful
for taking tack away from home. Get one that has a hook
which can be pulled out to hang it from the side of the box.

I have two pieces of tape attached to the inner hook.
I tie one loosely round the headpiece of the bridle, and the
other through the two terrets on the pad. I put the breaching
over the pad, and the breast collar on top of that.

The various straps hang down in the carrier. The reins slip into
the bottom of the carrier, or can be put in the pockets. (I have
found this much easier than the usual case or laundry basket,
as the pieces naturally come out in the right order when
harnessing up!)

Also for Carriage Drivers, a breeze block or equivalent
can be a useful way of balancing a carriage if adjustment on
your carriage is tricky and you only want a temporary change.

It can be easily moved (on a rubber mat if you are worried
about the paintwork) and will stay where it is put over all
but the bumpiest of terrain.

I have grooms of various sizes and weights, and the block
saves having to adjust the balance when giving 'rides'.

Elizabeth Lovick
Orkney

Was it good for you too?

Don't struggle to scramble up into the saddle from the
ground. If there's a mounting block available, use it! Ignore
comments from those who plainly don't know any better and
call you a wimp: just point out that it's better for you,
the saddle and for the horse's back too.

Karen Bush
Equestrian Author, Journalist and Riding Instructor

A clean slide

When cleaning a saddle to remove or replace stirrup leathers,
lift the back of the saddle up onto the pommel and the leathers
will slide easily in or out of their keepers.

Robin Porter
ILPH Field Officer

A clean coat

Grey or coloured horses whose quarters or hocks have
become stained with ingrained stable dirt, can be cleaned by
applying Swarfega or a similar product to the affected area.
Leave for five or ten minutes and then wash off with warm
water. If the area is still not perfectly clean, repeat
the process.

Tony Schorman
ILPH Field Officer

Language please!

'Would you throw a three year-old child into six feet of water and
expect him to swim?' Anita Yates, instructress, GMP, asked.

'No, of course not.'

'Then don't do it to your horse! They're exactly the same.
Now do it again. Gently. Show him exactly what you want him
to do, don't just sit there and expect him to understand.
Or don't you know what you're trying to do anyway?
What are you trying to do?'

'Well I was just...'

'Be precise! How on earth can you expect him to understand a
totally foreign language as well if you don't even attempt to
speak it clearly yourself?'

Jeremy James
ILPH Overseas Consultant

Trust the carrot stick

When dealing with spooky horses or when handling and backing young horses, we often find that we need octopus arms that extend, for example if you need to get a horse used to having his back legs touched. I use a simple piece of equipment which I call a 'carrot stick'. This can be an old whip or any stick with a colourful plastic bag sellotaped to the end of it.

Your horse's eyes will probably pop out of his head when he first sees it, but you can slowly bring it nearer to him. Then touch him with it, putting it quickly in front of him if he tries to shoot forwards and to the side or behind him if he moves in other directions. Soon you will be able to stroke him all over with it.

When he is happy with this, you can shake it above his back and then above his head and under his belly. He will learn very quickly that the best thing to do is stand still and that actually this monster bag is nothing scary. He will start to chew and breathe normally while you shake the bag violently all around him, stroking him with it reassuringly now and then.

I have found that doing this helps a horse put his trust into man, makes him less spooky and nervy, and helps him get accustomed to a rider's legs on his sides and body on his back much more quickly. There are many things you can teach your horse with a carrot stick (including stepping over it) and it costs nothing.

Kat Koukourakis
Ex Head Girl, ILPH Cherry Tree Farm

Shake, rattle and roll

When trying to clip a young or difficult horse, firstly, if it is safe to do so, let the horse see others being clipped and also shake a full matchbox all over the horse to get it used to a strange noise.

Liz Hatten
ILPH Mobile Promotions Officer

Sir Peter O'Sullevan
Daily Express, 1976

As every serious punter knows, there is more chance of an average Tattersalls bookmaker laying a horse to lose £1,000 in a bet than there is of him laying a dozen brown eggs.

Sir Peter O'Sullevan
Racing Commentator and Journalist

Out in the midday sun

My horse suffers with sunburn on his pink muzzle and, when I first bought him, I was getting through no end of sunblock. The more I put on him, the quicker he rubbed it off – he really hated it. I mentioned this to my vet, who suggested I buy a tub of Potassium Permanganate and drop a few grains of it into a small container of water, which immediately turns the water to a dark purple. If you paint this onto the areas which are susceptible to burning, the skin instantly turns into a reddy tan colour, which lasts for about three days. OK, he may look funny, but it really works as he never gets burnt now.

But just a word of caution: beware if your horse throws his head about while you are applying the solution, as you could find that you've gained a few large freckles for about three days! And it won't scrub off – believe me, I've tried!

Mrs S A Clarke
Suffolk

A shining example

For an extra shine in the show ring, run a shoe quick shine sponge over your horse, avoiding the saddle patch.

Liz Hatten
ILPH Mobile Promotions Officer

Recycling for your horse

Never throw old towels away! Always useful for rubbing down and drying wet muddy hooves.

Keep some baby wipes in the stable - especially if you drive straight to work from the stables!

Baby oil applied to the mane and tail will stop tangles and keep them soft!

Always soak your hay – however 'good' it appears.
Instead of a fork/shovel, wear thick rubber gloves for mucking out - it saves your back!

Georgina Bishop
Derbyshire

Chapter Three

A law unto themselves

They say the law is an ass, but you won't believe some of these crazy horse laws from around the world!

Sent in by ILPH New Zealand

Citizens are prohibited from buying, selling or trading horses 'after the sun goes down' in **Wellsboro, Pennsylvania,** without first getting the permission of the sheriff.

In **Schurz, Nevada,** they have an old law which prohibits the trading of a horse after dark.

In **Pee Wee, West Virginia,** people are prohibited from swapping horses in the town square at noon.

A unique law exists in **Pine Ridge, South Dakota,** where horses are banned from neighing between midnight and 6am near a 'residence inhabited by human beings'.

In **Pocataligo, Georgia,** horses are not allowed to neigh after 10pm.

Paradise, California, retains a most unusual law that says it is illegal for a horse to sleep in a bakery within the town limits of the community.

In **Sutherland, Iowa,** a law governs how horses may be seen when on streets during evening hours. The animal must always have a light attached to its tail and a horn of some sort on its head.

No rodeos are allowed in **Boone, North Carolina** as a town law states no man is allowed to ride his horse in a violent manner.

Female riders in **Clearbrook, Minnesota,** should be aware of this one, governing the heel length of a horsewoman's shoes. Any such woman can wear heels measuring no more than 1.5 inches in length.

A loony clothing ordinance in **Upperville, Virginia,** bans a married woman from riding a horse down a street while wearing 'body hugging clothing'. A $2 fine can be imposed on any female rider who wears clothing that 'clings to her body'.

In **Omega, New Mexico,** every woman must be found to be wearing a corset when riding a horse in public. A physician is required to inspect each female on horseback - the doctor must ascertain whether or not the woman is, in fact, complying with the law!

In **Hartsville, Illinois,** you can be arrested for riding an ugly horse.

In **Pattonsburg, Missouri,** according to the Revised Ordinances, 1884: 'No person shall hallo, shout, brawl, scream, use profane language, dance, sing, whoop, quarrel or make any unusual noise or sound in such a manner as to disturb a horse.'

A **Wyoming** community passed this one: 'No female shall ride a horse while attired in a bathing suit within the boundaries of Riverton, unless she is escorted by at least two officers of the law or she be armed with a club.' And it continues with this amendment to the original: 'The provisions of this statute shall not apply to females weighing less than 90lbs and exceeding 200lbs.'

A misworded ordinance in **Wolf Point, Montana:** 'No horse shall be allowed in public without its owner wearing a halter.'

A **Fort Collins, Colorado,** Municipal Code: 'It is unlawful for any male rider, within the limits of this community, to wink at any female rider with whom he is acquainted.'

West Union, Ohio: 'No male person shall make remarks to or concerning, or cough, or whistle, or do any other act, to attract the attention of any woman riding a horse.'

Abilene, Kansas, City Ordinance 349 declares: 'Any person who shall in the city of Abilene shoot at a horse with any concealed or unconcealed bean snapper or like article, shall upon conviction, be fined.'

1899 vintage law from **Waverly, Kentucky:** 'Any person who shall ride a horse in a public place while wearing any device or thing attached to the head, hair, headgear, or hat, which device or thing is capable of lacerating the flesh of any other person with whom it may come in contact with and which is not sufficiently guarded against the possibility of so doing, shall be adjudged a disorderly person.'

A 1907 **Cumberland County,** Town Statute reads: 'Speed while on horseback upon country roads will be limited to three miles an hour unless one sees a bailiff who does not appear to have had a drink in thirty days, then the horseman will be permitted to make what he can.'

A newly married man in **Kearney, Nebraska,** can't ride alone. The law states that he can't ride without his spouse along at any time, unless he has been married for longer than twelve months.

Figure out this 1913 **Massachusetts** law: 'Whosoever rides a horse on any public way laid out under the authority or law recklessly or while under the influence of liquor shall be punished; thereby imposing upon the horseman the duty of finding out at his peril whether certain roads had been laid out recklessly or while under the influence of liquor before riding on them.'

Male horse buffs in **Basalt, Nevada,** are prohibited from eating onions between the hours of 7am and 7pm while out riding. The law specifies only men.

Ice cream lovers beware in **Cotton Valley, Louisiana:** 'Citizens aren't allowed to eat an ice cream cone while on horseback in public places.'

In **McAlester, Oklahoma,** it's taboo for a woman over 235 lbs and attired in shorts to be seen on a horse in public.

It's illegal in **Marion, South Carolina,** to tickle a female under her chin with a feather duster to get her attention while she's riding a horse.

It's a violation of the law for a married man to ride on Sunday in **Wakefield, Rhode Island.**

It is strictly against the law in **Bicknell, Indiana,** for a man to leave his new bride alone and go riding with his pals on his wedding day. The penalty is one week in jail.

In **Bismarck, North Dakota,** every home within the limits of Bismarck must have a hitching post in the front yard.

Budds Creek, Maryland, has a law that prohibits horses from sleeping in a bathtub, unless the rider is also sleeping with the horse.

In **Headland, Alabama,** any man on horseback shall not tempt another man's wife. An unmarried horseman should not stop overnight when the woman is alone.

Legislation in **Bluff, Utah,** regarding the Sabbath: 'Women who happen to be single, widowed, or divorced are banned from riding to church on Sunday. Unattached females who take part in such outlandish activities can be arrested and put in jail.'

Chapter Four

I remember when...

A dinner serenade

At the King's Troop Royal Artillery's barracks in St John's Wood, every mealtime for horses is heralded by a trumpeter sounding 'Feed Up'.

A few years ago, during a quickly snatched quiet spell, a large group of the horses were sent out to grass. Because time was short and there was not the opportunity to 'rough off' the horses, it was decided that they should all be brought in, given a tea feed and stabled each night. But most of the horses had not been at grass for a while and when it came to bring them in on the first evening they were not interested. For over an hour soldiers tried everything to catch these suddenly wild animals. They were herded, cajoled, walked up to and walked away from. Feed tins were even rattled, but all to no avail.

Suddenly, a trumpeter appeared at the top of the field. He played 'Feed up' and all the horses turned, galloped up to the gate and were led in to their stables!

David Mountford
Head of ILPH Equine Operations

Little Nell

Little Nell was difficult to handle. She'd been badly mouthed, badly broken and regarded people with terror. She was hard to box, difficult to shoe, awkward to ride. But Norman Brown, Inspector, GMP (and now ILPH Chief Field Officer), liked her: he was the only one who did, and the only one who really knew how to ride her because Little Nell wouldn't have hard hands.

Norman maintained that for all her vices Little Nell was a basically sound horse, had no malice in her and that she would always look after her rider. No-one believed him. 'She's the very devil,' they'd say. 'Get yourself a remount, get a decent horse.' For many years Norman rode Little Nell, keeping her out of trouble though he knew she was accident-prone. She paraded for him, took him through crowds at football matches where bricks, broken bottles and stones were hurled at her. He took her through the miner's dispute, up and down motorways at the dead of night in horse boxes, unloaded her in darkness and then rode her through driving rain on straight eight hour rides.

As Norman's administrative duties gradually took up more and more of his time, he reluctantly spent fewer hours in the saddle with Little Nell. Others rode her, complaining all the time that she was an unpredictable creature, that you never knew where you were with her. Norman insisted she would never bring her rider down. The telephone rang early one Monday morning. Norman answered the call. A horse had been killed. Little Nell had been cut down by a forty tonner. When the truck struck her, Little Nell dropped her rider off her shoulder and rolled him to safety.

Jeremy James
ILPH Overseas Consultant

Leading from the front

Picture the scene: Grunwick's, a nasty lockout of workers, becoming more militant by the day. The Superintendent rides up and down the groups of mounted officers giving his orders. His final encouraging words are: 'Any officer who becomes separated and unseated from his horse will be returned to foot duty.' The horses wheel into line, move forward and immediately the Superintendent is lost in a seething mass of workers, unseated and not seen again for the rest of the day!

Robin Porter
ILPH Field Officer

An unusual picnic

My horse Caramello is an Andalusian Stallion, with the most beautiful nature. He is happiest when he's allowed to wander around untethered, although his naturally inquisitive personality does get him into trouble sometimes!

Recently I have had some work done on my house, which has meant teams of builders with lots of sandwiches. It didn't take long for Caramello to find the stashes of cheese & pickle, ham & tomato and tuna & mayonnaise and demolish the lot!

Anthea Turner
Television Presenter

Tractor ahoy!

I remember once I was riding a young horse on the road to get it some experience of the world and to introduce it to traffic for the first time. It's one of those jobs that can be quite difficult because you want to make it a good experience for a horse but you never quite know what you are going to meet on the way. Anyway, I chose a quiet lane at a quiet time of day and apart from the odd spook here and there and the odd rude motorist, my little horse was doing fine. We must have been out for about half an hour and were heading home when I saw a tractor approaching. Luckily it was quite some way in the distance and not travelling too fast, so I thought I'd use the time to look for a gateway to step off the road while it went by.

I looked and looked but there was no gateway to be seen. It looked like we were simply going to have to deal with the tractor by staying on the road. The tractor was much noisier and much bigger than anything we'd met earlier but I didn't see it as such a problem provided I could slow him down before he got too close. As the tractor got closer, I could see it had a loader on the front. It was one of those spike loaders that farmers use for stabbing big round bales of hay or straw to move them around the farm easily. This was not a problem because the tractor driver quite rightly had the loader high in the air and well out of harm's way. As he got a little closer still, I could feel my horse becoming slightly more agitated. It was really quite different to anything he'd seen before.

The tractor was now about 50 metres away and I thought it would help if I asked him to slow down slightly. I put my right arm out and with my palm down began to gently wave him down.

The driver, aware of the potential danger, responded immediately. Unfortunately my hand signal which I'd intended to slow the tractor down had been misunderstood by the driver and he didn't slow down at all. Instead he lowered the loader arms so that the spike was at perfect stabbing height. Oh my goodness!!!

I wanted to put my arm out and ask him to raise the spike to a safe height again but I was afraid he might think I wanted him to speed up. What a dilemma.

Anyway, with a bit of improvisation from me and my horse, we did manage to slow him down although he still passed with the spike low. Once we'd passed, I imagined my horse saying to himself 'Human logic... I'll never understand them.'
Anyway, needless to say, we got home safely in spite of the tractor driver's best intentions.

Michael Peace
Founder of Think Equus Method of Horse Training

Off the rails

Some years ago I got a call from a lady to say there was
a pony tied to a railing on the pavement outside a shop on the
Liffey Quays in Dublin. She had seen the pony at 10am when
going to work and it was still there when she was returning
from work at about 4.30pm.

As the traffic in Dublin would be very heavy at that time of
day I rang the Gardai, nearest to the complaint, and asked them
to look into the complaint.

In about half an hour I had a phone call from the Sergeant in
charge who was very amused as the pony in question turned out
to be a stuffed pony outside one of the Auction Rooms along the
quays with a 'For Sale' notice around its neck.

Tony Schorman
ILPH Field Officer

Tales of a novice trainer

The first racehorse trainer I worked for, Syd Kernick in Devon,
was a superb horseman. 'Sit still,' he was forever saying. 'Three
parts of the art of riding is doing nothing.'

Sir Mark Prescott Bt
Racehorse Trainer

A Midsummer's Nightmare

Set: A neighbour's 10-acre lush, grassy field

Time: A balmy summer's eve

Main Characters: Tiggy – a 35-year-old, grey, Welsh Mountain escapologist

Me – an actor, a little older than the pony and definitely grey as a result of the pony's escapades.

Supporting Characters: Absolutely no-one

Audience: Three passers by

Running Time: No idea at all – after two and a half hours it was too dark to see my watch

Need I say more – except that I shall probably never get as big a laugh from an audience again!

Tony Head
Actor

Watch your dismount

I remember once on a pony-trekking holiday when our
group came to a troublesome field gate, our teenage trek-leader
decided to dismount from her horse by the unorthodox method.
With no more ado she deftly swung her right leg in front of
her over the horse's withers ready to jump to the ground
(as athletic but reckless riders sometimes do!). But on
this occasion things did not go to plan!

As the young lady slid out of the saddle, the loose bottom of
her anorak jacket looped over the saddle and she was rudely
jerked to an abrupt halt in mid-descent leaving her dangling
against the side of her mount.

Though the poor girl tried to twist around to extricate herself, she found that she was securely trapped by her own weight and began to panic, crying out as she struggled helplessly like a fish on a hook.

Although her horse was a thoroughbred, luckily he just patiently pricked up his ears and peered around inquisitively at his rider dangling against his side.

As much as I wanted to rescue the poor girl from her dangerous entanglement, I was seized by an uncontrollable fit of giggles at the sight of this ridiculous scenario and regret to being worse than useless.

The situation was very critical because any further disturbance might well have startled her horse into bolting (had she been alone, the results might have been disastrous).

However, on this occasion a serious catastrophe was narrowly averted by the actions of a more sensible member of the group, a young man who happened to be on our trek-leader's off-side. With great presence of mind he calmly and quietly approached alongside the rear of the horse. There were some tense moments as our group of riders watched in stunned silence as the drama unfolded before them and the heroic trekker began tugging at the trapped jacket. At last, after several futile attempts, the jacket suddenly slipped free and with a great sign of relief our trek-leader dropped limply to the ground in an undignified heap – a painful, but nevertheless instructive, lesson on how not to dismount from a horse!

Barbara Egan
Middlesex

That old devil called Rufus

When I was eight at the end of the war, we went on our first
holiday to Cornwall and my father bought me the most beautiful
bay 12.2 pony, called Rufus, and I don't think I have been more
happy before or since. We went home by train and it was
arranged for Rufus to be sent by lorry. We got a telegram about
a week later, saying: 'Rufus arriving, walking, 9.30'. And I burst
into tears because I had a vision of my darling little pony walking
all the way from Cornwall and his little legs buckling under him.
Fortunately, my father rang up the owner and the telegram
was a misprint, and it was supposed to be 'Woking', which
was the nearest big station to us.

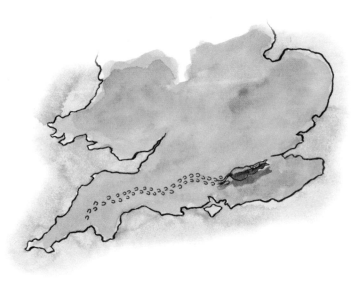

My parents went to collect him and I got home from school
and there was Rufus grazing quietly in our field. I was so excited
that I rushed into the field and flung my arms around him crying,
'Rufus, Rufus', whereupon he bit me sharply on the shoulder.
He was a beautiful pony, but he was an absolute little devil.
And apart from biting me at every opportunity, he had an
even more dangerous quality of folding up like a camel
and rolling whenever I got on his back.

We thought it would be better to take him out with other ponies
and he proceeded to mount the mare in front in the middle of
Black Pond Woods and we discovered he hadn't been properly cas-
trated. After that, I'm afraid he was sold. I was very, very sad and
felt I'd really let him down. Fortunately, my parents bought me
another very beautiful bay pony, called Willow, who stayed with
us for ten years, won masses of rosettes and was extremely satis-
factory and a darling too. But I've never forgotten Rufus.

Jilly Cooper
Novelist

A nun on the run

Way back in 1961, when I was a novice nun, I was allowed to pay a visit to my family in the New Forest.

It was a lovely sunny day, so we decided to go walking: my parents, my brother, my sister-in-law and me, dressed in the old-fashioned nun's black and white habit. With not a soul around, we were enjoying the dappled sunshine and birdsong, when suddenly a pony appeared, trotting at some speed.

My parents stepped back into a clearing, but the three of us started to run, because none of us were used to horses. My father shouted 'Stand still!', but panic had set in and we ran as fast as possible. Needless to say, the horse ran faster!

My brother and his wife were able to roll under a barbed wire fence to safety, but my clothes were long, full and cumbersome. I went on running, with the horse in hot pursuit. Into view came a gate.

I threw myself over the top, with all the agility of a 20-year-old, giggling hysterically with fright, and landed beside a couple sitting on a log enjoying the peace of the forest. They looked at me with pure astonishment. A lone nun behaving in a manner totally out of keeping. The horse was completely hidden from them behind a thick hedge.

I smoothed down my black habit, giving what I hoped was a decorous smile, and rejoined my family a little further along. My father said that, once I was out of sight, the horse calmed down and began grazing as though nothing had happened!

Miss Audrey Copping
Devon

'Fire bombs away'

When working on the miners' strike in the 80's on mounted duties, we were lined up in front of the pickets at Kiverton Park Colliery when the cry went out that fire bombs were being thrown by the pickets. Soon after, in the semi darkness, I saw a fire bomb missile come hurtling towards me and my horse. In stand by periods we used to play rounders using our staffs as bats (but I usually couldn't hit a thing). As the fire bomb approached, I made what I thought was a surprisingly good first class hit with my staff, fending the fire bomb away from my horse and myself. However, I was shocked to see that the bomb had landed on a colleague of mine and set him on fire. That colleague today is one of my fellow field officers, namely John Hodgson. He has never forgiven me for this incident.

John Pearson
ILPH Field Officer

Heavy duty horses

Lion and Violet turned left out of Hancock's Brewery yard,
then left again on to Wind Street, walked 150 yards and stopped
outside The No-Sign Bar. The drayman got off the wagon and
made his delivery of beer. The year: 1915. Lion and Violet
had been working together in harness for six years by then,
delivering beer round all Hancock's pubs in Swansea. But now
it was wartime, and the war demanded horses.

Lion and Violet were shipped to France in September that
year and faced their first winter through the canons and shells
and snow at Ypres. Together they pulled munitions wagons
over muddy French fields and along muddy French tracks from
ammunition dump to artillery line. Together they were sent to the
Somme and although Lion was wounded and Violet was forced to
pull the gun carriages alone, he soon recovered and together they
were set again to harness and saw action
all along the front line.

Three weeks after Armistice Day, Lion and Violet were
shipped home. Back in Swansea they were rested, fed and
tended back to condition since they had returned as you might
expect two Shire Horses to return after four years of war. When
they were put back into harness, a Dicken Medal hung from each
headstall. And the day they were put back to harness, the drayman mounted the dray, flipped the reins and Lion and Violet
turned left out of Hancock's Yard, then left again onto
Wind Street, walked 150 yards and stopped outside
the No-Sign Bar.

Jeremy James
IPLH Overseas Consultant

44

Captain courageous

My Grandfather was carter on a farm in East Sussex.
He loved his horses, and I think they must have
known it.

On this day, he had been out several miles from the
farm with two horses and the wagon. He was coming up a
steep hill in Winchelsea, East Sussex, and was teaming his
second horse, 'Captain' (in the shaft) through an archway near
the top of the hill. He was walking backwards and wearing a
long coat. He thinks he must have trodden on the back of it,
pulling him down onto his back. As he lay there he could see
the wagon wheel, which would have crushed him, coming
straight at him, but he saw 'Captain' look back at him
lying there and pulled over to one side of the road.
Instead, the only injury he suffered was to his
hand, where the wheel ran over it.

He said to his last day that 'Captain' saved his life.
I feel that is proof that being kind to your horse pays off in
the end. This happened before I was born and was told to
me by him when I was older. I am now 78 years old.

Mr C Harmer
West Sussex

45

Duke has the last laugh

Duke was an old Police horse, supposedly bought under
the guise of being a Shire cross, but we all knew that the cross
was probably another Shire horse. He devotedly patrolled the
streets of Sheffield day after day and his only real thrill in life
was feed time, or should I say 'Let's hit the ground with our
off-fore until the sparks fly!' time.

The officers were very fond of Duke and, because this
was his only fault, tended to feed him first at meal times rather
than rebuke him. His rider also adored him and, having been
in many scrapes together, would have nothing wrong said
about his trusty old steed.

One day at a local football match a crowd of quite drunk
and abusive football supporters gathered round Duke and his
rider and began to make fun of the horse's size and looks.
One of the youths held out his hand, containing a very large
mint, and placed it under the muzzle of the horse, but as Duke

was about to accept his offering, the youth pulled his hand away causing great screams of laughter from the crowd. The youth stepped forward again to repeat his trick, but as he did so an off-fore leg shot forward and caught the youth on the shin, sending him whimpering to the floor and creating even more laughter from his friends. The sweet fell to the floor and the officer released his grip on the reins to allow the horse to pick up his reward.

The youth, still wiping his eyes and rubbing his shin, shouted at the mounted officer that all horses were useless and should be replaced by intelligent Police dogs. 'Well if that's the case,' said the officer, 'he learns very quickly, because he was obviously trying to offer you a paw.'

John Hodgson
ILPH Field Officer

I had only worked for Jack Waugh as assistant trainer for about three weeks. I was leading a yearling who had just been broken out of the box to join the string. Mr Waugh was in the house 100 yards away, on the phone. The back door opened. 'Mark, take that in and take his temperature.' I did so and reported to the office that it was considerably raised at 103°C. This news was greeted with the comment 'I can see more from 100 yards away on the phone in the office than you can leading it – you've got a long way to go!'

Sir Mark Prescott Bt
Racehorse Trainer

The meat pie bites back

I was working a rather bad tempered football match in
Sheffield one Saturday afternoon, accompanied at the time by
another mounted officer who always helped the day go by with
his tremendous sense of humour. We had managed to separate
the minority of supporters who had caused the trouble, and
all were safely seated in the stands before we took up our
positions at the rear of the away supporters.

The whistle for half time meant an exodus to the tea bars
for the supporters and we generally mingled with them. A group
of about half a dozen youths, having bought their football meat
pies, gathered round my colleague and myself and started to give
their impressions on how we should really have policed the
match. One youth stepped forward and offered one of the horses
the remainder of his meat pie. The horse not being a meat eater
turned his nose up at the offering. 'There,' said the youth, 'even
your horses are unfriendly.' 'Its not that he's unfriendly,' said my
colleague. 'He just can't stand the thought of eating one of his
brothers.' The youth was last seen throwing his meat pie in the
litter bin, and dejectedly trudging off.

John Hodgson
ILPH Field Officer

48

They don't make them like
that any more...

In the old days when I was young, horses and ponies found to
have Sweet Itch were first washed thoroughly with a soap we
used to be able to buy called Carbolic.

The animal was then dried out. When dry, its mane and tail
were washed with a soap called Derbac soap, which was rubbed
well into the hair, but not swilled out, and allowed to dry.

When dry, the mane and tail were brushed lightly. Then we
puffed a powder into the mane and tail, parting the hair at the
same time. This powder was called Keethings Powder.

I am sorry to say that these products are unfortunately no
longer available. The Derbac soap was a black oval tablet.
The teachers at school used to use it when they found that a
pupil had lice in their hair.

I served my apprenticeship at a
colliery which in its early years had 300 equines, 90% of which
were ponies 12 hands to 13 hands in height and mostly under-
ground. These ponies never had Sweet Itch, and were looked
after and treated as well as racehorses.

I am going back to the 1929 – 1930 period when I first
started work.

Jill Doring
RSS, Warwickshire

Old war horses

'Jones' is the most famous Royal Horse Artillery horse. Colonel Main's handwritten history of Jones and Joubert - reproduced below - is kept at the King's Troop in St John's Wood.

The Story of 'Jones'
'J' Battery RHA 1914-1919
The Rocket Troop RHA 1914-1928

By Colonel A R Main DSO

'Jones' joined 'J' Battery RHA at Aldershot not long before the 1914-18 War. He went to war in the lead of a gun with 'Joubert'. The pair were together throughout the war, and were never 'sick or sorry'. In fact they were in the lead of the team of the gun that fired the first shell of the war.

After the Armistice they, among many others, were posted to the Rocket Troop in Germany. When I took over the Troop in 1919 they were in the lead of No. 4 Gun. In November the Troop came home and all our horses went into quarantine at Swatheling. From there we later marched up to Aldershot.

On arrival at the Square, knowing that we were going into the stables which 'J' Battery had occupied before the war, I told their drivers to let Jones and Joubert (by now renamed Othello) loose, to see where they went. They made straight for their pre-war stable and stalls. The last time that this grand pair of horses was on parade was at the unveiling of the Gunner War Memorial at Hyde Park Corner in October 1925.

David Mountford
Head of ILPH Equine Operations

Chapter Five

Rhyme and reason

Winter

Some people say we're strange,
folk like you and me;
We're out there with our horses,
whilst others drink their tea.

Deep in mud, deep in snow,
we're there through thick and thin;
It's our love for them that drives us on,
some find them rather grim.

But when we hear them munching hay,
or squealing with delight;
When they're rolling in the field,
or snorting loud with fright.

We realise why we sacrifice,
the comforts of the home;
There is no greater passion you see,
than for the beast that likes to roam.

**Remember: If winter comes,
can spring be far behind? (Old folk law)**

*Kat Koukourakis
Ex Head Girl, ILPH Cherry Tree Farm*

A pony has a nasty life
The ILPH come to give delight
To rescue the ponies from their fright
Take them home to treat them right
Let them sleep safely at night
For the rest of their lives

Anna Tolley
Aged 10

I saw your advert in the magazine
The most horrific sight I've ever seen
A poor grey horse in the ILPH advert
Caused me my distressed eyes to avert.

He's now in heaven in the land above
Where once again he'll find some love
What did he have down here on earth
All that mattered was 'what's he worth'?

A horse's life is worth more than money
Up in heaven he'll have bread and honey
His time on earth was full of pain
Up in the sky there's plenty of grain.

When a horse's life is over and done
He's reached the end, his time has come
He shouldn't travel, mile after mile
His end should come with comfort and style.

Roz Butterworth
Herts

Old innocence

Stained with rain
Round-rumped, conker-polished
Skin plumped
The bay gelding:
His dark body's gloss and solidity
A-swish and still
Neck bent to the feathery grass
Flower-summery.

His field companion
White, bony
Flanks concave, back sunken
Withers sharp, coat shaggy;
At thirty-two
Face still pretty.
Her eyes black lamps
Of deep wonder
As another day dies
And she still lives;
On thickened furry hocks
Stands by the fence -
A bit of the hornbeam for nibbling
Ash trees there when she wants them.

She catches a different light
Being all white -
In the evening
From the other one.

Caroline Ackroyd
Shrewsbury

For the love of horses

Dance like nobody's watching,
Love like you've never been hurt,
Work like you don't need money, and
Ride like you can't fall off.

Anon

To tell the age of horses

To tell the age of any horse
Inspect the lower jaw, of course:
The six front teeth the tale will tell,
And every double and four dispel.

Two middle 'nippers' you behold
Before the colt is two weeks old
Before eight weeks two more will come;
Eight months the 'corners' cut the gum.

The outside grooves will disappear
From middle two in just one year
In two years, from the second pair:
In three, the corners, too, are bare.

At two the middle 'nippers' drop;
At three the second pair can't stop
When four years old the third pair goes;
At five a full new set he shows.

The deep black spots will pass from view
At six years from the middle two
The second pair at seven years;
At eight the spot each 'corner' clears.

From middle 'nipper' upper jaw
At nine the black spots will withdraw
The second pair at ten are white;
Eleven finds the 'corners' light.

As time goes on, the horsemen know
The oval teeth three-sided grow;
They longer get project before
Till twenty, when we know no more.

From: Everybody's Encyclopedia of Things Worth Knowing, 1890

Contributed by Joan Barnard
ILPH HQ

Troy

A friend in need's a friend indeed
I'm sure you would agree.
But when human friends do come and go
You're still a friend to me,
It gives my heart a huge kick start
To see you safe and warm
And you know my friend, I'll strive
So you never come to harm.

I've never really thought about
the time you'll not be here
Cause Troy, my friend I hold you near in my heart
You're oh so very dear.
When people come and look at you
An old horse is all they see,
But what they don't seem to realise
Is that you mean the world to me.

Troy, remember what we have been through
All the good and all the bad.
But through it all, one thing shines bright,
We're the best friends we've ever had
So remember what you mean to me
And fight with all your might
For we've got the best to care for you
And he will put you right.
When you go to sleep my handsome Troy,
I'll be the last thing that you see
And the first thing that's in focus
when you wake up, will be me.

Paul Teasdale
ILPH Field Officer

Horses read our minds

If you think 'I can't catch him',
you won't.
If you think 'This lorry will scare her',
it will.
If you think 'He won't jump the jump',
he won't.
And if you think 'She'll buck me off',
she will.
But,
If you think 'I can catch him',
you will.
If you think 'This lorry won't spook her',
it won't.
If you think 'He'll jump this jump',
he will.
And if you think 'She won't buck me off',
she won't.

Always think positive – horses know what we're thinking.

Kat Koukourakis
Ex Head Girl, ILPH Cherry Tree Farm

Sally's pony

Sally rides her pony
For hours every day.
They walk and trot and canter
Along the bridleway.

Fences, hedges, ditches,
They fly them all with ease.
Sally sits there safely
Gripping with her knees.

She doesn't mind the weather.
Come wind or rain or shine,
Sally's in the saddle
At least by half past nine.

She doesn't shirk the grooming,
And cleaning tack is fun –
Not like some other girls
Who leave it all to Mum.

All this is quite surprising
'Cos Sally's only three...
The rocking horse is still
Just now,
While Sally has her tea.

Mary Darnell
Hants

Through the eyes of a child

A tear to my eye arose when,
Seeing my horses in this pose,
Granddaughter Elysha, nearly three,
Took my hand, looked up at me,
And said,

"Look, the horses are having a
cuddle, bless 'em".

Jean Brown
Warwickshire

Never too old

At the tender age of 63, I thought that I should try
To do something with my little horse, before life passed me by.
Cross country seemed a bit extreme, show jumping, well maybe,
But how about some Dressage, that could be the thing for me.
After all it cannot be so hard, if you can ride a horse,
You only walk, trot and canter around a given course.

I booked a lesson with Felicity, t'was then the truth emerged
The language it was foreign, I did not understand the words.
I had to use my inside leg, give with my outside hand
Get on the right diagonal and teach my horse to bend.

Felicity is going grey and tearing out her hair
But with her help and others, maybe I will get there.
I thought it would be simple, how wrong can someone be?
But now that I have started, I won't let it beat me.

I'll enter all the local shows, I will face the test
Though I may never be the tops, I'll always do my best.
And when I have to change my horse, to 'ride' a zimmer frame
I'll look back and smile and say, 'I enjoyed the dressage game'.

Jean Brown
Warwickshire

Chapter Six

And finally...

Twist in the tail

Behind every legacy that the ILPH receives lies a reason, and it
is usually due to the fondness that we feel because horses touched
our lives in some way. This story has a sad twist.

Miss Howarth of Hall Green, Birmingham, died a spinster
at the age of 92. Her niece, her executor, sent in her aunt's very
generous legacy, for which I thanked her. I do not usually receive
a reply but on this occasion the niece got in touch to say that she
wanted us to know that the legacy came about because of the sad
circumstances of her aunt having never married. Evidently, many
years ago she had met and fallen in love with a man who was
passionate about horses. Unfortunately, Miss Howarth did
not share this passion, so eventually he found and married
a lady who did!

Mrs Denise Sharman
ILPH Legacy Officer

Prayer said over Lord Lonsdale's Grave

O Father of all thank you for the dumb creatures,
which thou givest us, and which are the friends of man.
Give to us the understanding which may preserve us
from causing them needless pain.

Sir Peter O'Sullevan
Racing Commentator and Journalist

Changing of the Guard at Buckingham Palace

Before the days of railings and one-way traffic around
Buckingham Palace, mounted police were daily employed to
prevent visitors to the guard change from spilling out onto the road
stopping traffic. Japanese, French, German, American, every known
nationality, would disgorge from coaches in Constitution Hill
and fight their way to the front of the Palace to try and get
the best picture.

This young probationer mounted officer atop a fine chestnut
would spend two hours pushing tourists back onto the footway.
On a particularly fine day in May, easing the chestnut forward, a
Japanese man refused to move. More pressure and stronger language
was used and still he refused to budge, apparently shouting abuse at
the officer. Suddenly the tourist fell over backwards, his very
expensive camera sailing six feet into the air and crashing in pieces
onto the pavement. The officer looked down to see that the chestnut
had inadvertently been standing on the welt of the tourists shoe,
which had now come away from the upper leather. Feeling very
guilty, the young officer tried to assist the tourist, but he refused to
have anything more to do with the policeman.

A memory always returns to haunt the now not so young retired
officer that a claim of compensation could have been made against
him and his mounted career put in jeopardy, but most vividly of the
poor Japanese man returning to his coach carrying pieces of his
camera in both hands and the sole of his shoe flapping!

Robin Porter
ILPH Field Officer

Peculiar creature

Stabled in Knightsbridge Barracks, Quo Minus was a horse of peculiar habits. During feeding time, he would keep a few oats in his mouth, then dribble them out. As pigeons fluttered down to pick them off the floor he swatted them with his front feet.

Jeremy James
ILPH Overseas Consultant

Rolls of honour

It was the day of the Lord Mayor's Show. The procession was to be led by the Chief Inspector, followed by the second-in-command, both riding a pair of 17.2hh greys. A swords-on-day. The horses were steady and dependable. As the parade turned into the centre of town, the Chief Inspector on his grey made a half circle to the right, followed by the second in command. Both horses stopped and waited for the remaining horses to wheel and stand in line as the mayoral Rolls-Royce approached. It was a bright sunny day: horses gleamed, silver buttons glittered, plumes blew in a light wind.

The Rolls purred slowly through the crowds, the Lord Mayor waved regally, and as the car slid gently behind the Chief Inspector's grey, he stood on his front feet and kicked in every panel from bonnet to boot.

Paul Teasdale
ILPH Field Officer

Bird in the mouth?

A young girl came out of the crowd just before a football match and approached a mounted policeman. 'I know the name of that thing your horse has got in his mouth,' she announced with her pretty nose in the air. 'Oh?' asked the policeman. 'Yes,' she aired knowledgeably, 'a nightingale.'

Jeremy James
ILPH Overseas Consultant

Senior police officer's saddle club

Hyde Park police stables in the summer, always a pretty picture of flower boxes, tubs and hanging baskets, was looking particularly resplendent, when a senior officer, dressed in hacking jacket and bowler hat, attempted to mount his charger. Unfortunately, in his excitement at climbing aboard, he crashed his head onto a hanging basket wedging his bowler hat firmly down over his eyes and spilling the contents of the basket down his back. Whereupon the horse naturally thought it was time to go and set off with the unfortunate man, completely blinded by his hat and hanging on with both hands, unable to free the bowler. The horse, trained to perfection, completed two laps of Rotten Row and returned to the stable with the very shaken whimpering but unhurt Police Commander, who, to this day, has the distinction of having completed a morning ride without seeing a thing!

Robin Porter
ILPH Field Officer

About the ILPH

Who are we?

The International League for the Protection of Horses was founded in 1927, the main aim being to prevent the ill-treatment of horses exported to Europe for slaughter. It has grown to become the world's leading international equine welfare charity.

What do we do?

In Britain – In the United Kingdom the ILPH runs six farms dedicated to the recovery and rehabilitation of horses with around 300 equines in our care at any one time. Fifteen full time ILPH field officers, nearly all ex-policemen, investigate cases of cruelty and neglect, inspect markets and ports and also check the horses on the ILPH loan scheme. Thousands of rehabilitated horses and ponies have been found approved homes, and there are currently nearly 1,700 equines on the loan scheme.

Worldwide – Working in the developing world, the ILPH runs educational and training courses in saddlery, farriery, veterinary care and nutrition to combat the major causes of equine suffering and help the owners to help themselves.

We believe

In rehabilitation – the ILPH will attempt to return every horse that comes into our care to health, happiness and a good quality of life unless prolonging that life will only lead to further suffering.

In rehoming – any horse capable of an active life should be placed with a new loaner allowing us to take care of those new cases being rehabilitated. The ILPH retains responsibility for these horses throughout their life.

In education – it is better to provide knowledge than finance, as knowledge lives on after your departure. This principle applies to much of our international work.

In sustainable solutions – the ILPH believes in using locally available materials to allow permanent rather than temporary solutions to Third World problems.